Digital Results

The NO BS Approach On How TO Get Massive Results From Your Online Marketing, Avoiding Snake oil Tactics, And Build A Memorable Brand...

Presented By

Justin Burns & FunnelActive

Copyright © 2015 by Funnel Active
First Edition -

ISBN-13: 978-1508881117

ISBN-10: 1508881111

Produced by:

Funnel Active,INC
401 W. Ontario St. (Suite 225)
Chicago, Illinois. 60654

www.FunnelActive.com

Distributed to the trade by The Funnel Active Book Company

CONTENTS

ACKNOWLEDGEMENTS

Justin Burns would like acknowledge all of the members from the Funnel Active team who contributed to making this book a reality. Their expertise and valuable time has helped to make this book a valuable masterpiece for years to come. Thank you for all that you do to make an impact on this world.

INTRODUCTION

The Internet has been a game changer for many businesses; companies everywhere are trying to get a piece of the action and profit online.

Every company in the world, from the tech industry to the mom and pop local shop, knows the way to reach potential prospects; you need to know and understand what your prospects want.

As the Internet continues to shift and grow, constant competition and changes makes it even more challenging. The days of paying a web designer and putting a simple ad up are over. If you don't have a way to nurture and educate your prospects, you stand for your online business to go extinct. As more and more competition increases online, the simple advertise and hope for the best method will cease to exist.

I wrote this book after feeling sick and tired of seeing business owners waste money on out of date methods and things that only worked years ago.

So how will this guide help you? The answer is that it will help your business grow online, without the hype snake oil and B.S. I wrote this book after applying a proven repeatable formula we finally figured out to scale businesses online.

What you hold in your hands is something that will differentiate you from your competition and give you an upper hand. Whether you're a local business, online business, expert or just getting started, these strategies I lay out are only what I wish were available to my business when I got started.

More importantly, they're the strategies that have taken many companies from being on life support to thriving in any economy. Your customers are online and, if you want to thrive, you must meet them there. **Let's begin.**

1

ONLINE MARKETING DOESN'T WORK Anymore..."

Allow me to cut the bullshit and get right to the point.

For too long, honest online businesses have been sold "snake oil" when it comes to digital marketing.

Every day, I hear online business owners say things like, "online marketing doesn't work" or "online marketing is too confusing and I've been burned too many times."

This is because other online businesses have been promising the world and delivering nothing but oxygen. What's worse is that they've been charging the world for it and locking people into iron clad, long-term contracts.

Personally, I'm sick of it, I want to change it and that's exactly why I commissioned this study of successful businesses and put together this transparent, to-the-point report.

Now you're probably thinking, "who the hell are you and why should I listen to you on this topic?"

My name is Justin Burns and a couple of years ago I started an online company called Funnel Active. I raised it from the ground up with no investment from anybody else and grew it to become the online market leader in its industry while working with prestigious brands and clients from all around the globe.

The battles against other **competitors** gave me some sharp online marketing skills and when I removed myself from the corporate scene, I decided to start a digital marketing company dedicated to helping businesses like yours profit wildly online.

I've done digital marketing for myself, for my clients and I have personally managed millions of dollars for digital ad spend and, every single time, I've been able to make it come back with friends attached (ROI).

This book is put together from studying **200 successful online businesses** combined with my own real life experiences from being on the front lines of viscous digital marketing competition. My intention with my digital marketing company and this report is to be fully transparent.

Unlike other digital marketing companies who make things seem complicated and beyond your understanding on purpose, I'm going to show you exactly how things work and make things as simple as possible.

In this book, you'll find 7 things that successful businesses have in common when it comes to online marketing.

You can take these findings and implement them in your own business to start getting results almost overnight. This book starts by explaining "the digital marketing formula" and then provides three battle tested tactics in the areas of:

1. Getting more traffic (people visiting your website)

And...

2. Converting more traffic into customers

Stop what you're doing, get comfy and let's dig into the meat.

At the bottom, you have **CUSTOMERS**; people who buy your products or services either over the phone, in store or online.

The funnel itself is your digital marketing and its job is to CONVERT the traffic into customers.

When I studied 200 successful businesses, ALL of them treated their online marketing as a funnel and ALL of them were able to tell me their figures within a blink of an eye.

Over the next few pages, this book is going to show you exactly how you can do two things:

1. **GET MORE TRAFFIC.**

2. **CONVERT MORE TRAFFIC INTO CUSTOMERS.**

Those are the only two sides to the digital marketing equation and you're about to learn the 3 best practices from each.

Let us press on.

In any successful digital marketing strategy, there has to be a discovery phase that sets the <u>blueprint for a strong marketing plan</u>. To be honest, it can be quite a challenge to determine the starting stages of your digital marketing efforts when you're first starting on a new project.

There are so many pieces to the puzzle which typically leads in things either being rushed or being pushed to the side. This eventually leads to breaking deadlines and falling behind on your marketing.

You have to take the time to first get clear on your goals and objectives in order to have your team efforts aligned with the end goal in mind.

Many find themselves just doing "busy work" without really taking the much needed time to create a blueprint for the necessary action steps needed to accomplish your objectives.

You have to see the good, the bad and the ugly in every process to find the potholes and leaks in your current marketing plans.

So, what's the ultimate goal of a lead generation strategy?

The answer is fairly simple; your main goal should be to provide your customer with a product or service that fulfills their needs.

So, how are you going to get your product or service in the eyes of your customers?

Here is where lead generation strategies put you on stage to showcase your goods to potential customers. Some top digital strategies that never fail include SEO (search engine optimization), display advertising and PPC (paid search advertising), just to name a few.

Display advertising and content marketing are both great ways of generating a spike in brand awareness for your product or services.

Once you have acquired a new customer, you must be willing to invest time to keep them happy and engaged. The new shift in online marketing has changed the game around since customers can now seek and engage with your business during the buying cycle.

Using powerful content modalities that engage your audience via email marketing, social media and live webinars have proven to be effective in improving your capabilities in acquiring and retaining new customers.

Then, the next step is to decide which tactics are better aligned to hit your specific target market(s). Most businesses get overwhelmed by diving straight into the marketing without truly grasping the strengths, weaknesses and purpose of the strategies they choose to implement.

Contrary to popular belief, doing a little bit of everything is detrimental in your business. In the end, it's better to focus on doing three things great than doing twenty things poorly.

Furthermore, you have to find a common ground to align your strategies and end goal(s). For example, if you're focused on generating leads, you must find a system that works like clockwork to help you get leads for your business.

When you're focusing on a targeted list, you will yield the results that you're looking for. You will also find balance between quantity and quality. In short, content marketing is a great way to attract customer retention and generate leads which is the key component in any successful digital strategy.

You have to get your strategies aligned with the right tools such as the following; paid search advertising (PPC), display advertising, search engine optimization (SEO), social media marketing, video marketing, email marketing, conversion architecture, mobile marketing, etc.

The main point of this section is to help you not only discover your marketing plan but be able to invest less time while yielding massive results. It's crucial that the time invested is used wisely to not only identify but analyze your goals and objectives for your digital marketing plan to pay off in the long run.

This will position you to achieve marketing success in the online world.

Businesses that really want to have success with their digital marketing efforts online must be willing to become educated on new techniques and strategies which may be totally new to your team.

You have to be willing to educate your team properly before ad spend is used for any marketing campaign. Failure to do so may result in you having a hard time getting it to gain the proper traction needed to get you the desired results.

When it boils down to any type of digital marketing strategy being implemented, you must make sure that your whole team is on the same page. Everyone must be pulling in the same direction to avoid being slowed down by any bumps on the road.

As with technology, things can shift and change quickly so your typical medium of getting results can be outdated in a matter of months.

You should always be consulting experts in order to keep yourself up to speed on any recent changes since they're in the trenches as the internet landscape is evolving.

You have to find a healthy balance between your in-house team and the intricate creativity and expertise of your industry leader. In this market, you can't be afraid to be an **innovator** and think outside the box to get your company to the next level.

2

Think Like An Investor When It Comes To Traffic

Too often, digital marketing campaigns are setup and managed by creatives and this is a recipe for disaster.

Creatives are always trying to come up with new, exciting things and make things look beautiful instead of looking at the numbers, finding out what's working and then doubling down on that.

Instead of thinking like a creative, you've got to think like an investor!

Just like investing, with digital marketing, you must learn to ignore your emotions and make your decisions by numbers.

You're not "Coca Cola" or "Vodafone," you shouldn't be running so called "branding ads" to get your name out there. You should be running ads that bring you customers and a return on investment.

If somebody ever tells you that your ads are for "branding" or "getting your name out there," run for the hills.

Leave branding exercises to the big brands and the very demise of your own competitors.

Your ads should bring you customers and they should cost you less than what you make on the sale - that is all.

Creatives are always talking about cool new ideas, new designs, beautiful images or social media campaigns that generate "likes" when all they should be doing is getting you customers and delivering you $10 back from $1.

Let me ask you a question.

Let's say you're looking to invest some of your hard saved money in a company; are you going to choose the company that looks "cool" with no numbers behind it or the one that looks less exciting but has data to prove that it's going to grow?

You'd pick the one with the numbers.

The same is true in digital marketing - you've got to learn to think like an investor and keep the creatives on a leash.

When I studied the 200 successful businesses, they all treated their digital marketing campaigns like investments.

They knew that if they put $1 in here, $10 would come out 45 days later and they had all of the data to back it up.

There was no guesswork, no creative genius and no flukes. They had built their digital marketing campaigns to bring in customers and generate a return on investment and that was all.

Successful companies' digital marketing campaigns were run by people with an obsession with numbers. They tracked and measured everything you could possibly measure and they knew what happened to every single dollar.

So, what does all of this have to do with getting traffic to your website?

Well, traffic costs money.

Whether you're running Google Adwords, Facebook Ads, or paying a company to rank your website organically so that it comes up on the first page of search engines, it all costs money.

When you think like an investor, you try each one on a small scale, see if it works and then, if it does, you try spending more and if it doesn't work, you stop spending.

Let me give you an example.

We have a real estate client who started out spending $1,000 a month with us for Google Adwords. It took us 1 month to collect the data and we found that for every $100, we were generating him around $500 - a 500% return.

The next month, we upped the budget to $2,000. The numbers and the returns still held the same so we upped it again, this time to $3,000, and the returns were still the same.

Today, that realtor spends $10,000 a month on Google Adwords and in 1 year, she has grown from a 1 man business to a 10 man business and is making over $100,000 a month.

Did we create her a fancy logo or put a pretty image on her website?

NO. We thought like investors, started small, collected data, found what worked and then scaled up.

When it comes to digital marketing, chain the creatives to a tree, think like an investor and get a return on your investment.

A Website Is Just Not Enough Anymore

When you're thinking like an investor, you have to realize that a website is just not enough. You have to take time to invest in the right things such as your content marketing arsenal.

A typical, static four page website doesn't build trust of any kind, especially when you're trying to build a loyal consumer base.

You want to focus on volume with valuable content for SEO purposes in order to be able to rank well with Google and not raise any red flags that could penalize your site.

If you fail to add fresh and meaningful content, this will lead your site to poor rankings, no visibility on search engines and tons of headaches since you can't get your content to the masses.

Building a strong reputation is truly priceless in the online world. It could take months to build and you could lose it a split second if you're not careful to follow the rules.

Some traditional marketers still believe that "content marketing" is basically giving away something for free with no hopes of any return. However, if done correctly, you can build a strong list that you nurture to bring in a strong breed of loyal customers when you need it the most.

By taking the time to produce great content, you will see your business become a trusted and reliable authority with information that delivers a great sense of reputation when it comes to your products and services.

3

Content Marketing Makes Financial Sense To A Smart Investor

Sure, content marketing does require both time and money but it's undoubtedly the best vehicle when compared with other sources used in paid search advertising. Content marketing allows you to get up on stage and speak to the masses on a daily basis. Many take this medium for granted and it's a reason why their message is not getting anywhere.

There are a number of things one must take into account in order to have success with content marketing if you want to be a savvy investor.

The first one is getting web traffic to your site. If you have all of your SEO pieces aligned and you're posting quality content, your website metrics /analytics tool will help you to determine what is in demand as per your readers' engagement with your site. By taking the time to look at the numbers, you will know how to better cater to your audience.

The second one is the quality of sales leads you're bringing onboard. By targeting the right audience and publishing content that is meaningful to their needs, you will undoubtedly attract the right quality of leads to bring in sales to your company.

Third is the power of direct sales. By taking the time to build powerful content for your marketing strategy, you will start to build a loyal following. If done correctly, you will be able to enjoy reaping the rewards of direct sales so you know you're heading in the right direction.

Fourth is the listening to feedback from customers. Whether you're using social media or an online survey, it's crucial that you fully engage with your customer to get a better idea about their needs. They are also your best eyes since they can save you both time and money by pointing you in the right direction for certain things you might have overlooked in the process.

Taking the time to thank and reward them for a job well done will help you go a long way to show them that you care.

4

Multiple Streams Of Traffic

One is the most dangerous number in business.

Companies that depend on the number 1 are at extreme risk.

Let me give you an example.

A company has 1 client that pays them $1 million dollars a year. If that client decides to leave, they have $0.

A company that has 1,000 clients paying them $1,000 a year makes $1 million a year and if one client decides to leave, they still have $999,000.

Being dependent on 1 anything in business is dangerous.

The same is true with traffic to your website.

You don't want to be dependent on any one source because it could disappear on you tomorrow.

Let me tell you the most profitable sources of traffic:

- Organic Google Search

- Paid Google Search (Adwords)

- Facebook

- YouTube

All of these are awesome sources of traffic and each one alone can be responsible for driving you tons of new business but you don't want to be caught with a reliance on just one.

You want to build multiple streams and have your eggs in multiple baskets.

Now, another thing that most people don't understand is that one stream of traffic affects another and as you add them together, you begin to amass a cumulative effect.

Let me give you an example.

Let's say you test $1,000 on Google Adwords alone and find that it delivers you $2,000 back - a 100% return.

Then, let's say you test $1,000 on Facebook alone and find that it delivers you $2,000 back - another 100% return.

Next, let's say you test both together at the same time with $1000 on Adwords and $1,000 on Facebook. Your data would suggest that you'd see a return of around $4,000 but you actually see a return of $5,000 - this is the power of multiple streams of traffic.

One stream of traffic often compliments another and you see what's called a "cumulative effect" which boosts your return on investment.

This is why multiple streams of traffic can be so powerful for your business.

You not only cover your downside by eliminating risk but you also increase your return on investment beyond what you would normally see from one activity done alone.

When I studied the 200 successful businesses, all of them had multiple streams of traffic and none of them relied on just one. They used Google Adwords, Organic Google Search, Facebook, Youtube and others as well.

They were not at the mercy of 1 provider when it came to traffic and they took full advantage of the cumulative effect present when using multiple streams.

The point made here is a big one.

Don't rely on just one source. Take advantage of the cumulative effect of using multiple streams together.

I guarantee you that your competitors are not taking advantage of the cumulative effect in digital marketing. In fact, I bet that they don't even know what that word means.

As mentioned previously in this book, pay-per-click (PPC) ads can be found on all search engine results pages. The positioning and ranking on those ads is actually determined by your bids for specific keywords related to your product or service.

Keyword research tools are used to help determine which words are best suited to get you in the eyes of your prospects based on their search activity and behavior. A popular ad platform for Google is called Adwords. Competitors such as Yahoo and Bing have their own platform for PPC that you can deploy for your marketing strategy.

So, how does this work?

When a prospect clicks on your ad, they're redirected to the page that you have setup in the system. Google will determine that placement of your ad based on your budget and click-through-rate (CTR). There are more technical things that go behind this process but getting acquainted with this is very important.

So, should I worry more about SEO or PPC?

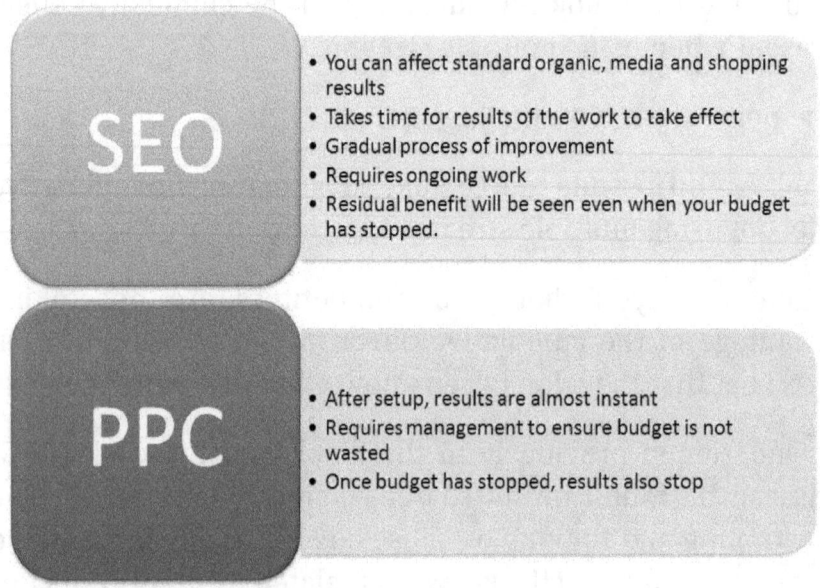

SEO
- You can affect standard organic, media and shopping results
- Takes time for results of the work to take effect
- Gradual process of improvement
- Requires ongoing work
- Residual benefit will be seen even when your budget has stopped.

PPC
- After setup, results are almost instant
- Requires management to ensure budget is not wasted
- Once budget has stopped, results also stop

This question really depends on many factors that are directly related to your marketing goals.

Let's talk about SEO.

Understanding How The Search Engines Work

Over the past ten years, the way the search engines work has changed significantly, especially with the introduction of the Google Map listings (Google Plus Local) to the search results for local search. A majority of the [Niche Type] we talk with are confused about how the search engines work and the differences between the map listings, organic listings & the paid / PPC listings.

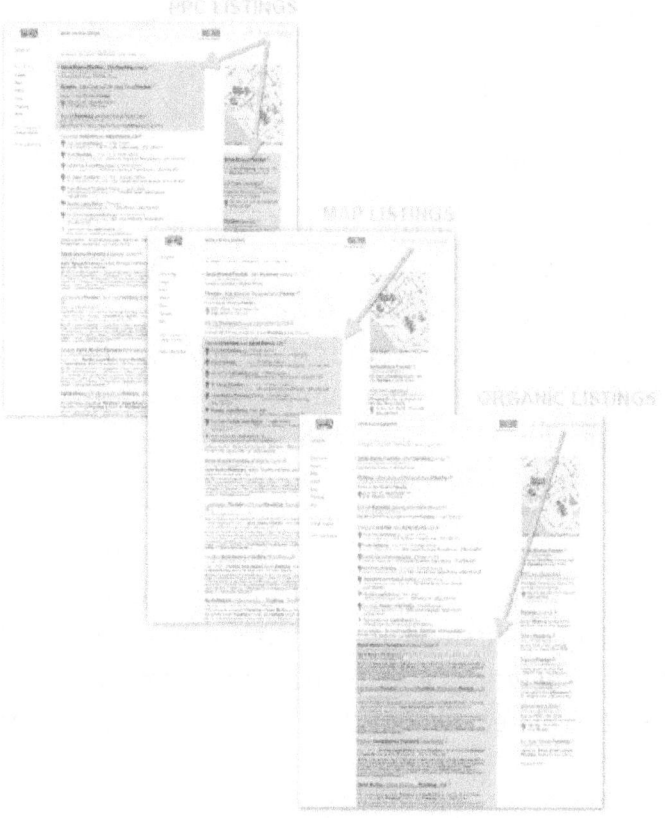

In this section, we wanted to take a few minutes to DEMYSTIFY the search engines and break down the anatomy of the search engine results page (SERPs). By understanding how each component works, you can formulate a strategy to maximize the results of each.

There are 3 core components of the search engines results page:

1. Paid / PPC Listings

2. Map Listings

3. Organic Listings

Paid / PPC Listings

In the paid section of the search engines, you are able to select the keywords that are relevant to you and then pay to be listed in this area. The reason it is referred to PPC or Pay-Per-Click is because rather than paying a flat monthly or daily fee for placement, you simply pay each time someone clicks on the link.

The PPC platform is based on a bidding system and the company that bids the highest gets the best placement. PPC is still a good way to market your business online but should be thought of as a short term marketing solution. PPC can get very expensive very fast with some keywords costing as much as $60.00 per click in the [Niche Type] industry.

Map Listings

The map listings have become very important because they are the first to come up in the search results for most locally based searches. If someone searches "[Niche Keyword] + your city," chances are that the map listings will be the first thing they look at.

Unlike the paid section of the search engine, you can't buy your way into the map listings, you have to earn it.

Once you do, there is no per click cost associated with being in this section of the search engine. We will share our Google Places optimization strategy with you later in this guide and show you exactly what needs to be done to obtain page one placement in the map section of the search results.

Organic Listings

The organic / natural section of the search engine results page appears directly beneath the map listings in many local searches but appears directly beneath the paid listings in the absence of the map listings.

The map section only shows up in specific local searches. Similar to the map listings, you can't pay your way into this section of the search engines and there is no per click cost associated with it. We will share our search engine optimization strategy with you in Section 5 of this book.

Now that you understand the 3 major components of the search engine results and the differences between paid listings, map listings & organic listings, you might wonder, "what section is most important?" This is a question that we receive from [Niche Type] companies every day.

The fact is that all three components are important and each should have a place in your online marketing program because you want to show up as often as possible when someone is searching for your [Niche Type] services in your area. With that said, assuming you are operating on a limited budget and need to make each marketing dollar count, you need to focus your investment on the sections that are going to drive the strongest return on investment.

Research indicates that a vast majority of the population look directly at the organic & map listings when searching and their eyes simply glance over the paid listings.

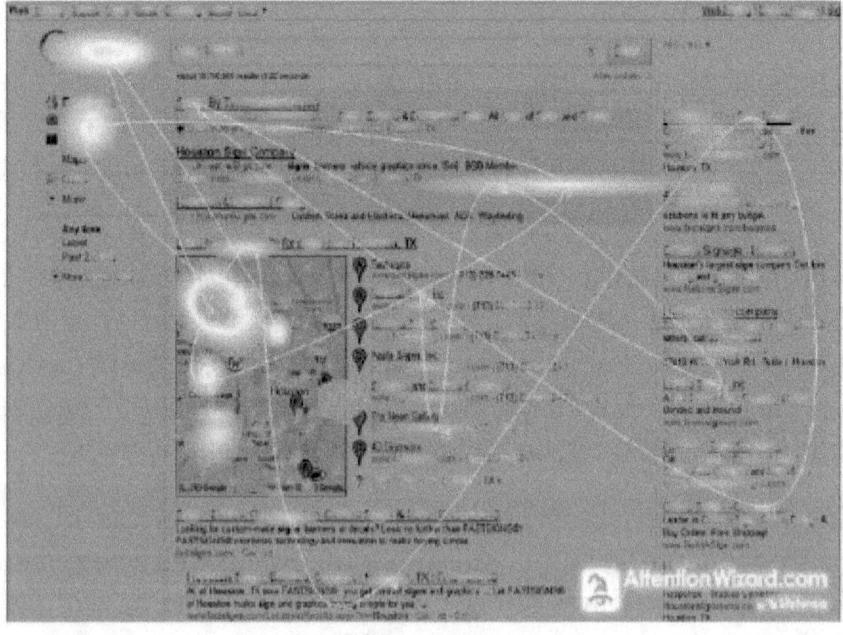

This heatmap indicates where the searcher tends to view as they come onto a search engine results page.

Where People Click On The Google Search Engine Results Pages

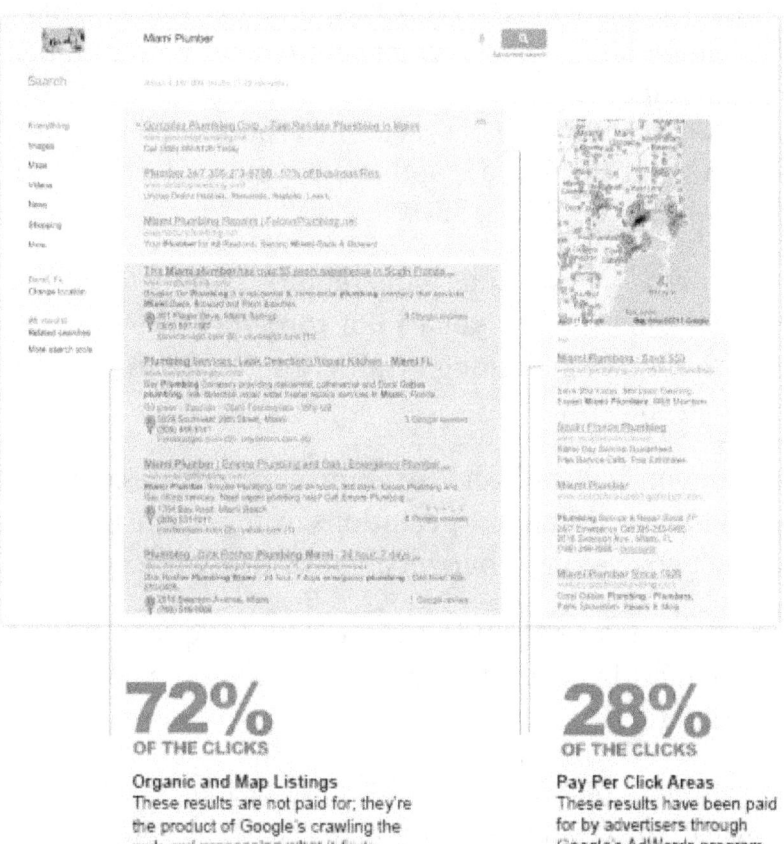

72%
OF THE CLICKS

Organic and Map Listings
These results are not paid for; they're the product of Google's crawling the web and processing what it finds.

28%
OF THE CLICKS

Pay Per Click Areas
These results have been paid for by advertisers through Google's AdWords program.

So, if you are operating on a limited budget and need to get the best bang for your buck, you should start by focusing your efforts on the area that gets the most clicks at the lowest cost.

There are many things to consider, such as:

- ➢ The competitiveness of your keywords and your actual budget.
- ➢ How much you're willing to spend for your PPC bids.
- ➢ The number of leads you need to meet your numbers or scale faster.
- ➢ The cost and type of service or product you're selling.
- ➢ How much money and time you can commit to spending on PPC & SEO.

Paid search advertising will require strategic keyword searches to make sure you're not throwing away money at things that don't get enough traffic. You will also need well-crafted ad copy.

Whether you have an in-house team or an outside copywriter, be sure that you set the expectations from the start to be sure you don't go over your budget as this can get pricey.

You will need your team to devote time to A/B ad testing to see which ad is converting best so you know where to put your money.

Your landing page copy, color and design along with a strong call to action strategy is also crucial as you piece your marketing puzzle together. And last, but not least, using Google Analytics tools to track the performance of your ad and individual pages will lead you in the right direction as you build a solid marketing campaign.

The beauty of traffic and fixed pricing

Unlike organic traffic, which can take some time to build with

SEO, you can get immediate results by doing paid search advertising. Your ads can appear on the first page of Google with the proper advertising management.

PPC is reliable and quick since it can be written and published in a matter of minutes. You have total control on when to run the ads and when to have them stop. You can schedule in advance to have total control over the date and times your ads can be seen on the web.

You can leverage the targeted PPC ad by target searches and even narrowing it down to a specific city. Google has tons of information to facilitate this process and allow you to get to your target audience quicker and reducing the guesswork.

PPC marketing has a lot of benefits to bring to the table. It's a driving tool that can bring positive results to your business daily if done properly.

Truth be told, there are billions of searches completed on a daily basis on all search engines which brings the much needed volume to hit your numbers with ease. When they're searching for specific products or services, they are leaving a trail-track which is relevant for your business.

This will allow you to find them quicker and bring your products and services to the comfort of their computer, tablet or mobile device.

When you have the right keywords in place, you will not find it hard to maintain a steady flow of targeted traffic to your website. You will be able to enjoy fresh or repeat customers to your website, searching for what you have to offer since you have taken the time to position it correctly based on their search behavior.

So, are you a dentist, chiropractor, lawyer, home improvement contractor, mechanic or local restaurant owner? Maybe you have a regional distribution enterprise or you're just simply starting out. Take the time to imagine all of the potential customers who are searching for services and products that you have at the moment.

So, where are they? They are going to your competitors instead.

PPC is just one strategy that can help bring customers back to you like clockwork. When a PPC campaign is setup correctly, you can expect to have a better pricing system that is consistent around your budget and needs.

Having multiple streams is just as important as what your content marketing has to offer. You want to make sure that you're driving traffic to valuable content that will eventually get you the sale.

It's simple to understand that the internet is the door for the initial search of your products and services. Aside from just word by mouth referrals, if you aren't on the web, you're missing out on many potential customers and that is the whole point of this book.

By providing top notch content, you will have relevant sources for many years to come and position yourself as the respected authority in your niche. By following the guidelines, you will get to communicate directly with your customers by means of a meaningful blog post, Facebook status or website survey, just to name a few.

If your PPC ads, SEO and content marketing strategies are consistent with your brand, you will attract new, hungry clients when they search based on their needs and land on your product or services.

It's not just about having a pretty website anymore. You need to communicate to your potential customers about your expertise, what you're working on and where you are headed so they can see you as the trusted visionary rather than some company that is inconsistent and all over the place with their marketing.

You don't want to be categorized as some company who is sending mixed messages to their audience. You have to take your online reputation seriously to be taken seriously for years to come if you want to build something meaningful with a great ROI.

5

Consistency Wins In Online Marketing

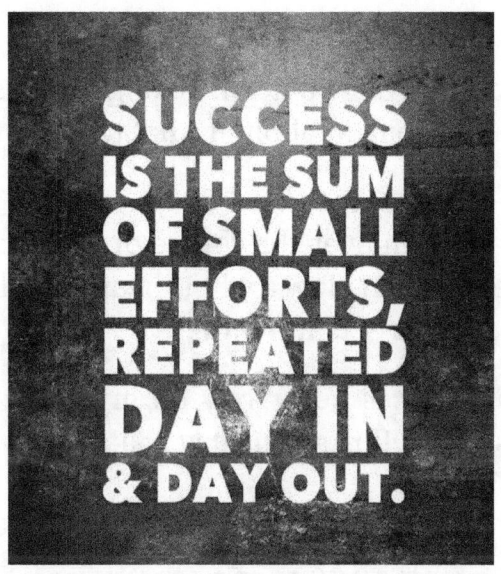

Business is not about "miracle efforts" or "miracle campaigns," it's about consistency and small efforts repeated day in and day out.

The same is true with digital marketing.

With digital marketing, too many businesses try to pull a rabbit out of the hat each month and create a marketing miracle when all they should be doing is focusing on consistent efforts every single day.

Creating an award winning digital marketing campaign for one month and then doing nothing the next is pretty much useless.

It's better to build a digital marketing campaign that delivers you a consistent flow of new business and runs day in and day out for the long term.

You want to build yourself a "digital marketing asset," something that delivers value on an ongoing basis. This way, you never need to pull a rabbit of a hat to make your nut.

It's much better to spend $1,000 a month on a digital marketing campaign over the course of a year and generate consistent return than blow a whole heap of cash in a hope of a miracle on one particular month.

Successful businesses never rely on miracles, they rely on proven, consistent efforts done day in and day out.

Let's take a look at the math.

Let's say you spend $10,000 on Google Adwords and Facebook one month while hoping for a miracle. I guarantee you that the most money you'll get back on that will be $10,000 at the very most - a return of nothing. Why? Because that's not the way digital marketing works. You need to start by testing small, gathering data and then start to optimize. You can't fluke it, it's a science.

Now, let's say you spend $1,000 on Google Adwords every month for an entire year. The first month, you'll probably break even because you're testing the waters and gathering data. Within the next eleven months, the return will continue to scale until you reach the campaign's optimum position. Over the course of the year, you'll spend $12,000 ($1,000 a month) and you'll get back anywhere from $24,000 to $240,000, depending on how good the person is managing your campaign.

So, a look at the two situations.

Miracle Month; best case is your money back with no extra gain.

Consistent Effort; anywhere from 100% - 2,000% ROI

When I studied the 200 successful businesses in United States, I found that none of them ever tried to pull off "miracle months."

They focused on proven, consistent efforts done day in and day out.

Their marketing budgets were never $10,000 one month and then nothing the next - they were evenly spread throughout the year with the exception of "high seasons" in some particular industries, such as the Christmas period for consumer products.

Successful businesses considered their digital marketing campaigns as one of their greatest assets.

Let me use one of my clients as an example.

We have a client that is in the dog training industry in United States and when I met them, they would do something different every single month to try to get customers in the door and turn inventory.

Some months, it was radio, some US herald, some prime time TV on stations like NBC and FOX. Sometimes, big 5 figure spends on Facebook advertising and Youtube.

Each time they did these campaigns, they got customers in the door and they turned the inventory which was great but the next month, they'd have to come up with something completely new.

I set them up with a digital marketing campaign that incorporates multiple traffic sources and delivers them what used to be their very best "miracle month" every single month without fail and with no guesswork, rabbit in a hat tricks or sleepless nights hoping things will work out.

6

The Hidden Truth About Online Marketing: Measure Everything Or Die

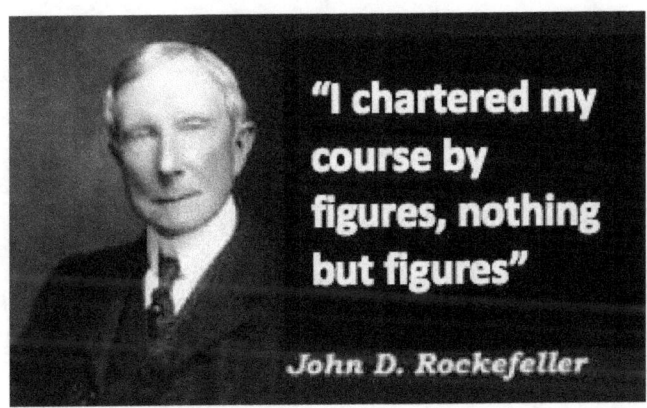

"I chartered my course by figures, nothing but figures"

John D. Rockefeller

The single most important thing in business is measurement.

John D. Rockefeller is without a doubt the greatest businessman of all time. He never made a loss in his entire life in business, even through the great depression, and he amassed a fortune of $340 billion dollars (1.5% of Americas total GDP).

John D. Rockefeller said this:

"I chartered my course by figures, nothing but figures".

Read that quote a couple of times. Think about it, let it really sink in. He didn't say he went with his gut or that he relied on intuition as so many of us do. He said he used nothing but figures to chart his course.

Numbers were Rockefeller's secret weapon and they're also your secret weapon when it comes to digital marketing.

The best businesses in the world can go bankrupt without good bookkeeping and accounting and so can the best digital marketing campaign.

If you're to take one thing from this report, please let it be to measure everything in your business and see what is actually happening with your marketing dollars.

I almost fall off my chair when I meet with people and they say they're spending $5,000 a month and have no idea what return that gets them.

I mean, how is that different from throwing $5,000 out the window and hoping it might do something?

It's not.

You see, without measurement, you don't know anything.

For all you know, you might be getting ZERO in return and your so called "digital marketing manager" is just pocketing the total sum as beer money.

Ridiculous you might say, but how are you to know when you don't have any figures?

When I studied the 200 successful businesses in United States, every single one of them had their eye on the numbers and that's how they made their marketing decisions.

No guesswork, no "let's go with our gut" conversations, just "here are the numbers and this is what we should do according to them."

Just like John D Rockefeller, these businesses didn't get rich by "luck," they got rich by charting their courses with facts and figures.

For every different channel of digital marketing, you should know the following:

Cost Per Website Visitor - How much it costs you to get somebody on your website.

Cost Per Email Enquiry - How much it costs you to get somebody to take the next step and email you.

Cost Per Phone Call Enquiry - How much it costs you to get somebody to take the next step and call you.

Cost To Acquire A Customer - How much it costs you to actually get a paying customer through a paid advertising channel.

Return On Investment (ROI) - The amount of profit you make when you subtract the cost to acquire a customer figure from the average revenue per customer figure - the return on your investment.

If you don't know all of the above metrics or if the person managing your digital marketing can't tell you, you seriously need to make some changes. You're essentially flying blind.

Why would somebody do digital marketing without knowing the numbers, you might ask?

Well, it can only come down to two things.

1. They just don't know.

OR

2. They don't want to because then they're on the hook to deliver when it's easier to just have you spend blindly. If this is happening, RUN.

Measurable Results = Increased Conversion

When you have launched your PPC campaign, you can start collecting data right away. You will be focusing on not just the number of visits or impressions to your site but the actual number of conversions which is your end goal. Your conversions can be tracked in several ways by achieving the following: download, sale, contact or subscription. In short, it's your end goal of what you're essentially trying to achieve with your ad.

For example, when we're giving away something to get an email in return, you can safely say that a subscription is our end goal for conversion purposes. From there, we go into doing email segmentation follow ups in order to build trust so that we can eventually offer them something in the future or right away.

It all really depends on what you want to accomplish with your marketing campaign and the effort that you're willing to put out in order to achieve that outcome.

Then, you will study your data to make improvements in your PPC campaigns. Not all PPC campaigns are created equal so you must take the time to really study and master your craft to truly set yourself apart from the competition.

You essentially want to convert your search traffic into customers by checking the performance of your ads and making changes where needed. Taking the time to measure the click-through-rate (CTR) of your ad conversion rates will help you reach higher numbers for optimum performance.

You have to be open minded and willing to experiment with new ads, change the text, tweak the headlines and look at the overall design. When you're running multiple ads simultaneously to see which one performs better, this is known as A/B testing. You have to be willing to test a bit out of your comfort zone to see which ads can convert best so you put every dollar into good use.

Again, you want to test variations of special offers, texts and calls to action for best results. You want to give them what they want then tell them what they need. Be clear and to the point on what they will get when they click on your ad and what incentive you will reciprocate by having them take certain actions on your site.

When someone opts into your newsletter or giveaway, they are essentially trusting you with their information because they believe that you will deliver the goods. Having a great copywriter will allow you to work wonders, even when ad space is limited. You must be smart enough to utilize all of your tools to get the job done.

Take the time to track the performance of your keywords.

Study with your team the raw data to determine which keywords are the ones driving traffic that is actually converting to your site. Dump the ones that don't add up with results and bank on the ones that have proven to get you results.

By devoting valuable time in studying these numbers, you will find other keywords that are related to your searches that you never thought about before because of your broader search tactics in the beginning of your campaign.

Sometimes you will surprise yourself by going from broad to narrow and vice-versa to get those special keywords that people tend to overlook. You will be able to see your CTR go up and your costs go down to help meet your budget goals.

What are you trying to accomplish?

When you place a PPC ad and someone goes to your website, you must be focused on what things are important in your business when this takes place. So, what are you trying to accomplish?

This is going to vary depending on your company needs

that we mentioned earlier. Do you want them to request an appointment, fill out a form, join a mailing list, download a free report or just pick up the phone and call you for a free strategy session?

Again, all of these are types of website conversions that you want to track individually with your team. How hard is this? It's as simple as inserting a tracking code into each page that you want to monitor so you can measure everything. You can't fix what is not measured and you can't grow if you don't know your numbers.

There are tons of tools out there to help track your ads and specific keywords in your campaign. These will allow you to weave out the converting ones from the others which aren't getting you any results.

As you continue to apply these principles and learn new things, you will adopt many things that you see work for your digital marketing initiatives to make your business soar to new heights.

The magic key to these strategies boils down to managing and measuring the results of your campaigns. It's plain and simple but many of your competitors fail to acknowledge this for lack of patience and tools to get the job done.

You have to enter the world of web analytics with a humble but hungry heart to yield the results that you're looking for in your business.

Everything will be determined by the amount of hard work you or your team is willing to put into each marketing project.

Once you understand how to analyze, measure, collect and interpret all of this data, you will optimize your web experience for maximum results. Measuring is what successful businesses do day and night. The numbers don't lie when you look at your company's financial reports. If you fail to do so, it's the same if you ignore your digital marketing data.

Everything will build upon each other to get you from point A to point B. If you're not marketing efficiently, how do you expect to get more sales?

Nowadays, you can't afford to neglect data since it could be costing you money. Your web analytics data will have to be broken down to choose the most relevant results to study since it can be a bit overwhelming at times. If you have hired a traffic or ads manager, be sure to always keep your eyes on the numbers instead of false hopes and ideas that can be luring you away from your end goal.

By making sure that your data has proper quality, relevancy and accuracy, you can rely on data that is congruent with your website and daily marketing activities to reach your goals.

Please be sure that you start measuring everything from the start. You need to be able to successfully measure, analyze and compare your marketing campaign results to see the health status of your marketing strategies.

You need to determine what is measuring up to your numbers to see improvement or abandon ship on things that seem to be great but are actually wasting your marketing dollars.

Like a good investor, you're looking for the best return on your investment.

Websites have many objectives as seen below. See which one meets your needs.

For example, in an **e-commerce website**, your main goal is to get visitors to buy directly online; it's a one way street.

In a **content website**, the goal is to get visitors coming back for more when it comes to consuming your content.

Then, you have a **lead-generation website** which is essentially created to get all visitors to enter in their contact information so that you can turn these prospects into customers with time by getting them to know / like / trust you.

And lastly, we have the **customer-support website** where you give them the answers they need by allowing them to contact you via call or chat options on your site.

These four types of sites will help you in identifying your business objectives. You want to be sure that your site is easy and user-friendly. The last thing you want is having customers browse for long periods of time to get answers because they will find them on other sites that took the time to tailor to their needs.

Also, be sure that your goals are aligned with 3 key things in regard to your analytics: acquisition, behavior and outcomes.

Your campaigns must be timely, useful and relevant to provide the best metrics for your business goals. Be sure to segment your data into different groups in order to better analyze and make fast decisions when implementing changes. Be sure to think "outside the box" when you're analyzing the data so you can make your own custom changes as needed.

On the web, you can find endless resources on how to do almost anything or you can always seek the help of an analytics professional if you get stuck in the process. You can always rely on tools such as Google Analytics to setup your campaigns and track what you need. Rest assured that you can always export this to mediums like Excel or PowerPoint for easier reporting tactics.

Marketers and business owners should always have a reliable way to track, set goals and measure all of your marketing initiatives to build successful campaigns to get the best return on their investment.

Whether you require a bit of offline and online tactics to get visitors to a digital or physical location, you will yield the best results by measuring every step of the process. Everything else will fall into place as you go.

7

The Power Of Sales Copy That Helps Convert Prospects Into Lifetime Customers

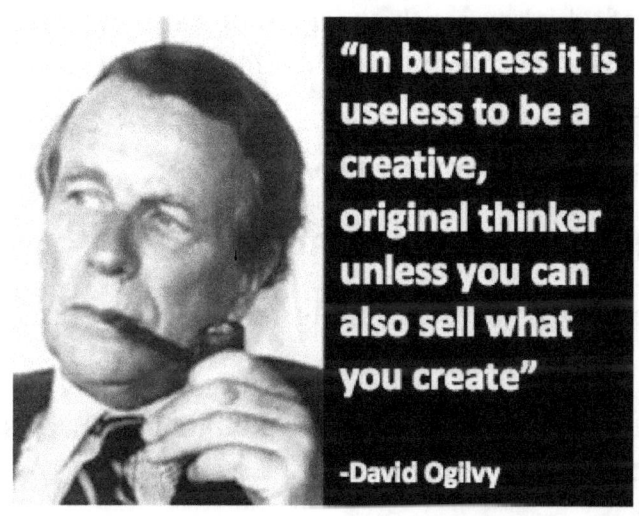

"In business it is useless to be a creative, original thinker unless you can also sell what you create"

-David Ogilvy

Here I go again, bagging the creatives.

Don't get me wrong, they're important people and I have nothing against them or their profession but they have absolutely no business being at the helm of your business' digital marketing with your wallet in hand.

A creative will tell you that this image should be this big and needs to go there because it looks good, NOT because it will bring you more customers.

Creatives have an eye for what looks good, what's in fashion and what's pleasing to the eye, not what makes your phone ring, makes people come into your store or puts dollars through your till; for that, they don't have a care in the world.

Your website isn't a fashion piece, an art show or a vain contest of who has got the best looking site in your industry. It's a conversion piece, a vehicle for converting traffic into customers.

Remember the formula I told you about?

TRAFFIC X CONVERSION = SALES

Well, your website is the thing that does the "conversion" part.

Without conversion, you just have a bunch of useless traffic and a hole in your bank account.

One of the greatest advertising men of all time is David Ogilvy.

Ogilvy said, "in business, it is useless to be a creative, original thinker unless you can also sell what you create."

And he was right.

Your website isn't a brochure, it's a mini salesman talking to somebody and influencing them to take action and buy from you in the form of written words on a digital page.

When it comes to converting traffic into customers, WORDS ARE YOUR SECRET WEAPON.

Think about it, when you're in the market to buy a particular product and you start checking out different suppliers' websites, you're hungry to learn. You're hungry to see if what they've got solves your problem, takes away your pain, gives you the life you want and has been proven to do it for others.

Now that's what a website should do.

Get people's attention, show them that what you've got can help them in their situation and get them the life that they want. And how do you do that, you might ask?

You do it with words.

Your absolute best sales pitch for your product should be the words written on your website. In the US, all of their websites had words that got people's attention, engaged them, handled their objections and then got them to buy.

When I studied those 200 successful businesses, all of their websites had words that got people's attention, engaged them, handled their objections and then got them to buy.

Just like a salesman, except in the written word on a website.

So, who wrote the words on these successful businesses' websites?

Well, it wasn't designers or some "web design shop" full of hipsters on Mac computers. It was either the business owner or one of their best salesmen; somebody that knows your customer and the conversation going on inside their head, somebody that knows why people buy your stuff, how to prove you're better than the competition, handle objections and get them over the line.

It makes me cringe whenever I see somebody remove words that help make a sale in order to fit in a nice looking image. That action is one of somebody who cares for how a thing looks and not for how much money will go through your till.

Your website is not a brochure or a vanity piece - **it's a salesman**.

A good salesman always delivers since customers are looking online for products, services and solutions to their most pressing problems.

It's up to you to be first in line to snatch those hungry customers first before the competition can get to them. Believe me, there is a huge market of competitors who are doing that right now as you're reading this book but don't panic because you will get a piece of the pie if you follow all of the valuable content shared in this piece.

You have to first realize that content marketing is really about understanding what your potential customers are searching for and the length of time spent searching for these answers.

There are four things that you must understand to deliver great content in bite size pieces to your audience.

First, you must put yourself in their shoes to <u>understand the challenges</u> that your current market is facing. You need to identify this targeted group so you can deliver the much needed goods in a special way.

Second, you have to be able to <u>solve their problems</u>. Don't just make it about you but take the time to really make it about them while making them see you as the obvious solution. This can be achieved by not just focusing on your value when it comes to your services and products but the actual problems that your target niche is facing and how your content is able to bring a solution.

Third, you have to **become a trusted authority** in your niche. You want to be the "go-to guy" (or gal) as the key trusted source of information. By publishing great content, you position yourself to build a strong and loyal following that will trust and respect you dearly. This is accomplished by providing content that isn't fluff and cuts straight into the meat by providing a solution to their most pressing problems.

Fourth, you must <u>provide fresh content to make it easy to buy</u>. By providing a great article or blog post, you can grow your authority over time using clever SEO tactics. You want to make the buying process as easy as possible for the potential customer. Things like your contact information, products, services and any relevant information must be easily accessible at all time. You don't want to make your prospects jump through loop holes to get to what they need. If you're quick at delivering the pathway to the goods, you will have an easier transition in getting the sale.

If you take the time to continuously provide online content, this will only build more streams for your ideal customers to read, trust and find you online. Adding clever social media tactics into the mix will allow you to better track your efforts through solid engagement modalities.

Measuring things like the number of shared Facebook posts or retweets for your content will help you see what campaigns are generating the most traction as you continue to grow by testing the waters.

In the end, the main goal of your content marketing strategy is to generate leads and keep your customers actively engaged. This is only achieved by providing free and useful information to position you as the authority in your niche.

The secret sauce is to make your website more about the customer. If you fail to let the customer know that you cater to their needs as your upmost priority, it will be harder for them to trust your product and will set them on opposites sides when looking for raving fans or advocates.

You always want your marketing to be consistent with your brand.

If you find a way, or several ways, to engage with your audience on a more personal level, you will have no problems with winning their hearts and votes. You can think outside the box to get more creative as you interact with your prospects and loyal customers.

If you find yourself with more than one target audience, you need to create custom content for each buyer. You have to identify the top three visitors who are typically on your site. Put yourself in their shoes and think about what information you may find interesting, useful or relevant to make you stay and actually purchase a product or service from the site.

What information can you provide to them in order to make their buying decision quick and easy? You always want to custom tailor your most valuable content to the target market that visits your site on a daily basis. By doing this correctly, it will translate into more sales for your business.

What makes your product different from the rest?

How does your support set you apart from your competitors?

There are clever ways of answering one part of the equation in order to later give them the whole formula to land the sale. Give them what they want and then tell them what they need

In terms of marketing, be sure that your SEO and keywords are relevant to your marketing campaign. Even if you have you need a birds-eye-view, this will allow you to determine what elements are in alignment with your customers needs at all times. (Odd wording, not sure how to fix properly, please clarify)

Be sure to define your ideal customer, understand your customers' most pressing problems, create awesome content and make it fun for the readers.

Also, take the time to find the ideal social networks for your potential customers. Are they on Facebook, Pinterest, Twitter, YouTube or LinkedIn?

Don't waste more time; create your ideal social media profiles to get your content in the right hands and start to grow your business with more qualified customers.

8

NO MARRIAGE ON THE FIRST DATE

BUY NOW, CALL US NOW, COME INTO OUR STORE NOW.
These are the words of too many businesses shouting in a market filled with noise.

Let me ask you a question.

If you were on a first date with somebody and you didn't know anything about them and suddenly they dropped to one knee and asked you to marry them, what would you say?

You'd say no.

Why?

Because you don't know enough about them, you don't trust them, you haven't even been given significant time to see if you like them.

So why do so many businesses ask you to **BUY NOW** or **CALL NOW** before first gaining your trust and providing value?

It bewilders me.

No human being calls you, comes into your store or decides to buy before first trusting you, liking you or your company and knowing that you're the right one to fulfill their needs.

So what do you do?

The same thing you do when you want to marry somebody; you start small with low resistance offers and then as you build a relationship, you start to progress through more engaging offers.

BUY NOW or CALL NOW is like "MARRY ME."

However, enter your email address here for more information on the topic of XYZ is more like, "hey, would you want to go on a date?"

Some people will still reject the offer but a heck of a lot more will take it over the BUY OR CALL NOW offer.

And that's what you do, you create a low resistance offer in exchange for some basic information and then start the relationship from there.

When I studied those 200 successful business, they all had low resistance offers to capture their prospects' basic information and began the relationships.

Successful businesses offer their market useful information on a topic that they know they're interested in, completely in exchange for some basic information.

What sort of useful information could you provide your market?

Well, here's how you should do it properly.

People don't buy a drill because they want a drill, they want a hole.

So, if you were selling drills, you'd offer people useful information on making holes. Get it?

Think not about your specific product or service but the problem it solves for your customer and then create a piece of information on that topic and offer it on your website in exchange for some basic information.

Out of **100** people that come to your website, only 3 will be ready to buy - and they will - but what about the other 97?

Well, that's why you have a lower resistance offer - to get their information so that you can market to them so that when they're ready to buy, they buy with you.

You have to realize that advertising is the art of getting people to buy things they don't need with money they don't have. Although this statement might seem a bit out there, don't doubt that there is some truth as you read between the lines.

People on the web rarely land across a website without a trail of searching behavior that has got them there. If you have the goods, it's your duty to help people on the web find it.

However, many websites are just poorly constructed, static pieces of clay positioned online just for the sake of having a website. People scan rapidly online so you have anywhere between three to nine seconds to persuade them to stay on your site.

Anyone who is willing to share their contact information with you knows that you will eventually try to sell them something. However, by positioning yourself as the expert and nurturing your prospect, you will make the buying decision much easier when they're ready to buy now.

How can I make my landing page sexy?

Great converting landing pages used to collect your prospect's information share the next three things:

1. **Awesome Content**: You have great and relevant content to back up the goods that you're offering on your site. You want to be able to get them to know, like and trust you.

2. **Sweet Incentives**: Give awesome things away. Whether you're giving a free report or a 14-day-free-trial, be sure to make it sweet so they can opt-in and share it with their family and friends.

3. **Super Convenient**: Have you ever read a good post and wanted to print or share it with the world? Where the heck are the share buttons? Be sure to include a one-click link to the most popular social media platforms (Facebook, Twitter, Pinterest, Google+, Instagram).

You can always improve sales by increasing traffic, up-selling and improving your conversion rates.

How can I make my landing page design a success?

There is no right or wrong answer as this really depends on your specific niche and goal. You have to make it not only your own but be able to achieve the goals that you want it to in the least amount of time.

Again, you have take time to define your customer. Make it appealing to the eyes of your target customer. This can be accomplished by determining their age, sex, ethnic background, income and anything else relevant to your ideal target. You can then take the time to craft a message that resonates with them in a special way.

Next, you want to select different domain names aside from your main homepage. This will allow you to have other custom and keyword rich domains to create your PPC ads and establish a better SEO presence online.

You also want to create a blueprint of what your page will look like. Where is your logo? Top left? Where is your phone number? Top right? What about your main headline, the image, the three main features, the form and call to action buttons? Are you also adding testimonials to enhance the credibility factor?

How is your copywriting? Words are everything so you must be sure that your copy is top-notch on your headline and bullet points. You must be able to trigger those emotions and provide a solution to their problems quick and easy. You call to action button must be displayed at all times to be sure that they don't leave and move along the process.

By testing and tweaking different pages based on the data from your analytics, you will be able to pick the winner. It must always be congruent with your goals to yield the best results.

Here is a quick rundown on elements typically found on high converting landing pages and website:

- conversion button
- logo
- headline
- countdown timer/expiration/deadline
- tagline
- video
- testimonial
- offer
- incentives

In regards to the copy, you must make sure that you have the following:

A headline that matches the original headline in you PPC ad, straight to the point text, keep your bullet points and paragraphs consistent and be sure that you use a combination of capital and lower case letters and spacing to make it easy to read and digest information.

One of the things that can kill your campaigns are things like the following:

- ➢ Adding too much text in your headline or bullet points.
- ➢ Broken links that don't work in your page and break the funnel sequence.
- ➢ Too many required fields.
- ➢ Missing email privacy/anti-spam policy.
- ➢ Lots of links leading to other pages that cause distraction and error with delivery date/pricing structures.

In short, landing page design, just like with any page in your website, requires a great deal of psychology. Keep your designers on the design and your IT guys on the programming. These are two different worlds and your job is to find a common ground so you can achieve success with your website. Below is a complete website checklist to help optimize your website.

YOUR COMPLETE WEBSITE CHECKLIST

Ideas for getting your website ready for the search engines and advertising online

Domain name & URLs

Why this is important: The domain name is part of the identity of your business. The URL chosen can have a significant impact on brand identity and in a lesser extent, keyword ranking performance. However, how your site domain name and page URLs function can have significant impact on the crawl ability of the site, as well, as overall visitor and traffic performance.

_ Short and memorable

_ Uses Keywords

_ Used in email addresses

_ Uses Favicon

_ Site.com redirect to www. version:

_ Alternate Domain redirects

_ Home page redirect to root

_ No underscores in filenames

_ Keywords in directory names

_ Multiple pages per directory

_ Registered for 5+ years

_ Multiple versions:

• .com

• .org

• .net

• .biz

_ Hyphenations

_ Misspellings

_ Product names

_ Brand names

_ Type-in keywords URLs

Site Logo

Why this is important: The logo lends directly to brand identity and site identification. It also creates a certain element of appeal and professionalism in the mind of the visitor. It holds an important role in visitor assurance and navigation.

_ Displays company name clearly.

_ Isn't hidden among clutter.

_ Links to home page.

_ Unique and original.

_ Use tagline consistently across site.

Design Considerations

Why this is important: The site design is essentially the first impression that someone gets when they land on your site. You may have all your usability and SEO elements

in place, but if the design is lacking then your visitor's impression of you will

be lacking, as well. A visually appealing site can not only bolster trust and credibility,

but it can make you stand out among other less-appealing sites in your industry.

_ Instant site identification

_ Crisp, clean image quality

_ Clean, clutter-less design

_ Consistent colors and type

_ Whitespace usage

_ Minimal distractions

_ Targets intended audience

_ Meets industry best practices

_ Easy to navigate

_ Descriptive links

_ Good on-page organization

_ Easy to find phone number

_ Don't link screen captures

_ Skip option for flash

_ Consistent page formatting

_ No/minimal on-page styling

_ Avoid text in images

_ Font size is adequate

_ Font type is friendly

_ Paragraphs not too wide

_ Visual cues to important elements

_ Good overall contrast

_ Low usage of animated graphics

_ Uses obvious action objects

_ Avoid requiring plugins

_ Minimize the use of graphics

_ Understandable graphic file names

_ No horizontal scrolling

_ Non-busy background

_ Recognizable look and feel

_ Proper image / text padding

_ Uses trust symbols

_ Works on variety of resolutions

_ Works on variety of screen widths

Architectural Issues

Why this is important: Website architecture can make or break the performance of a website in the search engines. Poor architectural implementation can create numerous stumbling blocks, if not outright roadblocks, to the search engines as they attempt to crawl your website. On the other hand, a well-implemented foundation can assist both visitors and search engines as they navigate through your website, therefore increasing your site's overall performance.

_ Correct robots.txt file

_ Declare doctype in HTML

_ Validate HTML

_ Don't use frames

_ Alt tag usage on images

_ Custom 404 error page

_ Printer friendly

_ Underlined links

_ Differing link text color

_ Breadcrumb usage

_ Nofollow cart links

_ Robots.txt non-user pages

_ Nofollow non-important links

_ Review noindex usage

_ Validate CSS

_ Check broken links

_ No graphics for ON/YES, etc.

_ Page size less than 50K

_ Flat directory structure

_ Proper site hierarchy

_ Unique titles on all pages

_ Title reflects page info and heading

_ Unique descriptions on pages

_ No long-tail page descriptions

_ Proper bulleted list formats

_ Branded titles

_ No code bloat

_ Minimal use of tables

_ Nav uses absolute links

_ Good anchor text

_ Text can be resized

_ Key concepts are emphasized

_ CSS less browsing

_ Image-less browsing

_ Summarize all tables

Navigation

Why this is important: A strong, user-friendly and search engine friendly navigation is essential in helping people and bots through your site. Your visitors need to find information quickly with minimal hunting and the search engines need to be able to follow the navigation to reach all site pages with the fewest number of jumps (clicks) necessary. If the navigation is broken or doesn't get people (or search engines) where they need to go, the performance of a site will suffer.

_ Located top or top-left

_ Consistent throughout site

_ Links to Home page

_ Links to Contact Us page

_ Links to About Us page

_ Simple to use

_ Indicates current page

_ Links to all main sections

_ Proper categorical divisions

_ Non-clickable is obvious

_ Accurate description text

_ Links to Login

_ Provides Logout link

_ Uses Alt attribute in images

_ No pop-up windows

_ No new window links

_ Do not rely on rollovers

_ Avoid cascading menus

_ Targets expert and novice users

_ Absolute links

Content

Why this is important: Content is an essential part of the persuasion process. Pretty, image-based sites may be appealing to the eye but it's the content that appeals to the emotional and logical centers of the brain. The inclusion of content as well as the effectiveness of the writing are all crucially important to the sales process.

__ Grabs visitor attention

__ Exposes need

__ Demonstrates importance

__ Ties need to benefits

__ Justifies and calls to action

__ Gets to best stuff quickly

__ Reading level is appropriate

__ Customer focused

__ Benefits and features

__ Targets personas

__ Provides reassurances

__ Consistent voice

__ Eliminate superfluous text

__ Reduce/explain industry jargon

_ No typo, spelling or grammar errors

_ Contains internal contextual links

_ Links out to authoritative sources

_ Enhancing keyword usage (SEO)

_ Date published on articles/news

_ Web version of PDF docs available

_ Consistent use of phrasing

_ No unsubstantiated statements

Content Appearance

Why this is important: Great content can get lost if it's not easy to read or if it is thrown into an otherwise cluttered page. Ensuring that your content fits visually into the site is just as important as having good content to begin with. If you want the sales message to get across, your visitors will need to read it.

_ Short paragraphs

_ Uses sub-headings

_ Uses bulleted lists

_ Calls to action on all pages

_ Good contrast

_ No overly small text for body

_ No overly small text for headings

_ Skimmable and scannable

_ Keep link options in close proximity

Links And Buttons

Why this is important: Links and calls to action are a great way to allow visitors to navigate from page to page, finding the information they feel is important to helping them make the purchase decision. Without these calls to action, many visitors will simply not know what they are expected to do next.

_ Limit the number of links on a page

_ Avoid small buttons and tiny text for links

_ Leave space between links and buttons

_ Avoid using images as the only link

_ Link important commands

_ Underline all links

_ Accurately reflects the page it refers

Home Page

Why this is important: The home page is often the single largest entry-point. It is the page that gives the visitor the sense of who you are and what they can expect. Go wrong here and it can be all over before it begins.

_ No splash page

_ Instant page identification

_ No Flash

_ Provides overview of site

_ Site purpose is clear

_ Robot meta: NOODP, NOYDIR

About Us Page

Why this is important: Studies have shown that conversion rates for visitors who have visited the About Us page increase measurably. Those who visit here are looking for a few extra elements of trust that will help them decide whether to continue on or move on. What they find can mean the difference in a conversion or the visitor leaving your site for a competitor's.

_ Adequately describes company

_ Shows team biographies

_ Shows mission statement

_ Up to date information

_ Note associations, certifications and awards

_ Links to support pages:

_ Contact page

_ Investor relations

_ Company news

_ Registration info

_ Job opportunities

_ Newsletters

_ Link to social media profiles

Contact Us Page

Why this is important: Those who land on this page are showing clear intent in wanting to to get in touch with you. Providing only a few ways to contact you can alienate visitors who have a particular preference. Providing robust contact options and information ensures that you capture as many would-be customers as possible.

_ Easy to find

_ Multiple contact options:

_ Phone

_ Fax

_ Email

_ Form

_ Chat

_ Customer feedback

__ Street map

__ Hours of operation

__ Final call to action

__ Multiple points of contact:

__ Customer service

__ Tech support

__ Inquiries

__ General info

__ Job applications

__ Billing

__ Management team

__ Ad-free

__ Form requires only essential info

Services Pages

Why this is important: The services page has a very singular focus. Its job is to provide the visitor with the information about the service they need to be convinced that it is exactly what they are looking for. If your service pages cannot convince visitors to call, you're simply dead in the water.

__ Visible calls to action

__ Clear contact info (phone #)

_ Consistent layout

_ Clear service presentation

_ Guarantee info

_ Service description

_ Customer reviews

_ Clutter-free page

_ Service Areas

Help And FAQ Pages

Why this is important: If your customers are digging through your help and FAQ pages, chances are that they are close to making a decision to purchase and they just need a little extra bump.

_ Avoid marketing hype

_ Link to additional resources:

_ Customer support

_ Q & A

Privacy And Security Pages

Why this is important: While most visitors won't read privacy and security pages, they do provide necessary assurances that visitors look for in terms of being able to trust you. However, when visitors do click into these pages, certain information needs to be presented to them to ensure their needs are met.

__ Present info in easy to read format

__ Provide section summaries

__ Identify information types collected

__ Explain how cookies are used

__ Explain how user information will be used

__ Explain how info will be protected

__ Link to these pages in footer

__ Provide links to contact info

There you have it. Make sure you go through this checklist and don't overlook any of these. Going through and making sure you have these are crucial for your online success. Let's get into the meat of what we talked about and now go into the digital checklist.

9

YOUR DIGITAL MARKETING CHECKLIST

By now, you should know that digital marketing is not some mystery exploration or "spend and pray" type of thing; it's an exact science that has a proven formula.

I have taken the time to create a "Digital Marketing Checklist" that you can use to make sure that your business' digital marketing is on the right track and in the hands of somebody who actually knows what they're doing.

If you check all of the boxes, congratulations, you're on the right track and the person at the helm of your business' digital marketing knows what they're doing! Hold on to these ones, they're rare!

If you can't check all of the boxes, please take this as **serious warning.**

You should have the numbers and you should be making a return on your investment of at least 2:1 - 200%

If you don't have the numbers, you're literally throwing money in the bin and if your provider doesn't have them or refuses to give them to you, they either don't know what they're doing or are trying to hide their pitiful efforts and so called results.

This book and check list is going to piss off a lot of digital marketing providers because I know for a fact they don't do it properly and they never will because its labor some and difficult. The mere thought of having to check these boxes and prove ROI to their clients would make them run for the hills.

No longer will honest businesses be sitting in confusion as so called digital marketing companies piss their money in the wind laughing.

You now know what works online and you have this checklist as your tool to grade their efforts.

Use it to your advantage and to your competitor's demise.

THE DIGITAL MARKETING CHECKLIST

Do you do digital marketing consistently all year round?

Do you have multiple streams of online traffic?

Do you have a numbers oriented person managing it?

Do you treat your digital marketing like an investor would?

Does your website perform like a mini salesman using words?

Does your website have a low friction offer to capture emails?

Has your website been built to convert traffic into customers?

What's your cost per website visitor?

What's your cost per email enquiry?

What's your cost per phone enquiry?

What's your cost to acquire a customer?

What's your average revenue per sale?

What's your return on investment?

Is your return on investment over 100% ($2 back on $1)?

If you or your provider can't answer all of the questions above or produce more than a 100% ROI then you need serious changes to your strategy.

Lead generation and customer retention are the keys to your business' competitive advantage. At the end, the lifeline of all companies is their ability to generate new sales and repeat business from current customers. These things are key in order to allow your company to grow.

Email is a tool to help generate new leads and nurture existing ones as your database continues to grow. Nearly everyone uses email and it's the most prolific way to reach your users in a matter of seconds. If you take the time to setup a direct marketing strategy by scheduling specific messages during a set time frame, you have the power to get them to like, know and trust you.

All of this will help make the buying experience much smoother. You don't have to spam or send email blast saying "buy me now" because that simply won't work. You have to take the time to nurture this relationship and let it blossom with time.

They say that the money is in the list, so the success of your email marketing list will be based on the quality of your list. Are you actively engaged with them? Have you build trust with them? What products have you recommended? What valuable content or services have you provided?

If you're on the phone, you can ask for their email address. You can also remind them to subscribe while on your website. You can provide an incentive (lead-magnet) to get them to subscribe by providing something of value for free, you can run a contest or help them share it on Facebook for an early bird discount.

Be sure to use a CRM to segment your list so you can, for example, separate the customers from the non-customers.

This will allow you to run separate promotions based on their needs. If you have different levels of memberships in your programs, this will come in handy to get then to upgrade to the next tier and not confuse the first time buyers with no memberships.

It can be fun and you can get creative along the process.

Email marketing is essentially all about relationship management. That list is your life-line of potential customers so you must use it wisely. You have to support, encourage, help and develop a meaningful relationships because all this will lead to sales now or down the road.

Be sure to take the time to create nurturing content to be delivered in bite-size pieces to your list so you can reap the rewards of building a loyal list.

Keep your emails short and to the point. Be sure to add a link directing them to a specific page on your website or video testimonial which they may find useful. If they need that extra push, be sure to give it to them with strategic marketing tactics. Also, be sure that your content matches your buyers and the purchase stage in which they are currently on.

Relevancy is the main key to your content which will build a stronger relationship with you and allow them to make their next purchase with you as opposed to the competition.

Putting the digital puzzle together.

At this point, you're probably a bit overwhelmed with all of the information we shared in which we avoided a lot of technical things to get our main messages across. We really understand how you feel right now. Digital marketing changes constantly, like the a new cell phone model at your nearest retailer. However, by devoting a couple of hours a week, you will be able to keep up and master a lot of information. We also understand that for many business owners, your time is very limited and your time is best spent doing the things that you're good at, like running your business.

Working with a FunnelActive team expert will allow you to keep doing those things and letting us put the digital puzzle together for your business.

Our goal is to prevent you from doing these things which will not only take your time but extra money down the road since it's not your primary area of expertise. We always say that it never hurts to seek for help from the experts when you're in doubt.

Not all digital marketing strategies are created the same. Unfortunately, this book can't really tell you which strategy will work best for your campaign. We want to leverage this with you to allow you to dominate and gain a huge edge over your competition.

HOW WOULD YOU LIKE TO DOMINATE YOUR MARKET AND GET A $10,000 DIGITAL MARKETING STRATEGY FOR FREE?

How would you like to dominate the market you're in?

How would you like to be found above all your competitors online?

How would you like to have a reliable way to generate a flood of new business every single month without ever having to pull a rabbit out of a hat?

How would you like to have a digital marketing asset where you knew that if you put $1 in $10 would come out?

I've got good news for you...

For a very limited time FunnelActive is offering a custom tailored digital marketing strategy for selected businesses.

You'll get to sit down with us and he will personally look at your market, your business and your competition and then create a custom digital marketing plan highlighting EXACTLY what your business should be doing in order to **dominate the market.**

This isn't a fancy way to try and sell you anything... This is pure value with absolutely no obligation and, quite frankly, it's a "no brainer."

At the end of the strategy session, if you don't believe you got at least $10,000 worth of value, then just say so and we will personally give you a check for $100 for wasting your time.

Justin has started and grown two companies into the millions, he's personally managed over $10,000,000 worth of digital marketing spend, has helped dozens of clients dominate their markets and is the author of this report.

Justin usually charges $1,000 an hour for strategy sessions and for a very limited time you can get one for **FREE** with **absolutely no obligations.**

It's pure value and you will leave the session with a custom tailored digital marketing strategy that you can execute yourself or hire somebody else to execute for you.

To claim your strategy session please call

312-600-7098 to schedule a time or click visit the url below to schedule a strategy session direction.

>> funnelactive.com/schedule <<

To Your Success!

—Justin Burns & The Team at Funnel Active

Justin Burns is an author, speaker and co-founder of FunnelActive, an online marketing agency that helps experts and businesses get more traffic and grow their businesses online. Justin didn't get his start on the Internet by just helping business owners. He has launched many successful businesses online; everything ranging from software (Saas) to information products, eCommerce businesses, and many others. He helps business owners with his services and consulting at:

www.funnelactive.com

Produced by:

Funnel Active,INC
401 W. Ontario St. (Suite 225)
Chicago, Illinois. 60654

www.FunnelActive.com

Distributed to the trade by The Funnel Active Book Company